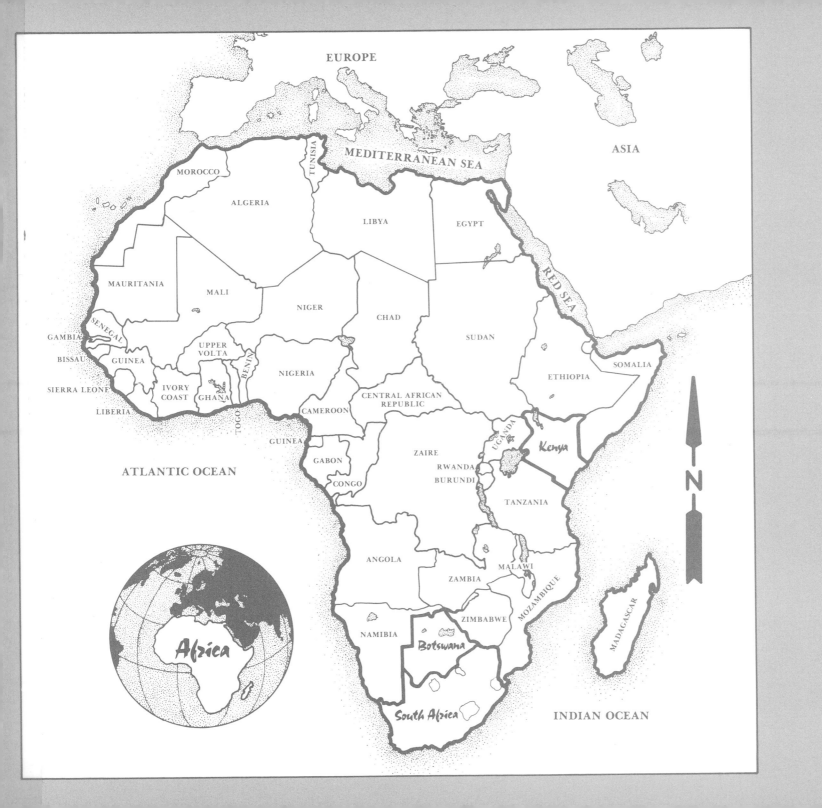

On Safari

dogs are the excuse

By Nancy-Carroll Draper

On Safari
dogs are the excuse

By Nancy-Carroll Draper

Photography by Nancy-Carroll Draper
Book Layout & Design By Tim Stamp
Edited By Jon Messmann

Published and Printed By:
Rustler Printing and Publishing, Cody, Wyoming

Library of Congress Catalog Card Number: 84-61038

ISBN 0-930535-00-6

Manufactured in the United States of America.
First Edition First Printing 1984

Dedication

To my Mother, Ruth Carroll Sharp
A lover of animals and
a conservationist at heart

Introduction

Conservation is an attempt to make man conscious of the flora and fauna and to give him the interest essential for preserving and enhancing the wildlife and wilderness.

It is beauty and glory. It is a living heritage to be protected, respected and nurtured.

These pictures are but a small effort to capture the images of the unspoiled wilderness that is still a part of this African continent. They represent a heritage which must be preserved, for as Emerson said, beauty is its own excuse for being.

Nancy-Carroll Draper

Dogs are the excuse for so many things, the reason for so many wonderful and positive parts of our lives. Dogs have been the excuse and the reason for firm friendships, for love affairs, for business partnerships, for new directions in one's life. Men have met their future wives through dogs, and left some because of dogs. People have found new friends and new worlds through dogs, and dogs are the reason that brought me to undertake these photo safaris into mystical, magical Africa.

Of course, dogs have always been a part of my life, having founded Danelagh Kennels in Ridgefield, Connecticut some 40 years ago. My family was amongst the earliest breeders of Irish Wolfhounds in America as well as Labrador Retrievers and English Springer Spaniels. As an approved American Kennel Club judge of Great Danes for the past 15 years, I have been honored to judge at all the major shows in the United States including the Westminster Kennel Club in New York, the International Kennel Club of Chicago, the Santa Barbara Kennel Club in California, the Kansas City Kennel Club and the Westchester Kennel Club in New York. I have also judged in Canada, England, Sweden, Ireland, New Zealand and Australia.

It was perhaps only a natural result of these activities that I was honored to be asked to judge in Africa, and since that first invitation I have judged the South African Ladies Kennel Association, the South African Great Dane Association show, the "Westminster" of South Africa, the Goldfields Kennel Club all-breed show and the Great Dane Club of East Africa. But to go to these magnificient places without taking advantage of the other natural glories of these and their neighboring countries would be tantamount to going to a superb restaurant and eating only a breadstick. My life with animals just would not permit it!

On these pages are recorded my impressions of the wildlife of these magnificient countries. I have seen, observed, recorded through eyes conditioned by a lifetime of breeding, raising, showing and judging dogs, as well as breeding cattle. I hope I have been able to bring something extra to these impressions, to capture through the wildlife, that combination of vastness and intimacy, power and beauty, that is the contradictory essence of Africa.

Kenya

The Ark

. . . . passing notes.

Green. Dark green and light green, deep, brooding and vibrant, shimmering green, shadowed green and suntouched green, every shade and tone of green imaginable with a red ribbon of a road running through the thick forest.

The Ark, that's what they named this place, for, like the original Ark of Noah's, it is a repository for almost every kind of animal, a refuge, a place of relative safety. But the Ark is a lush place, latent with life, bursting with creatures great and small. They are everywhere and everyplace, defying the eye to find them all. Up high, Colobus monkeys pause to look down in between their swinging leaps. On the ground, a Cape Buffalo grazes unbothered and unperturbed, a Bushbuck darts off into the thick foliage, the swift and the slow, the stolid and the nervous, predator and prey, they are all here in this Ark.

One climbs to reach this place, a seemingly endless climb, up to an altitude of some 8,000 feet. You are closer to the sun and yet the sun is filtering light, sifting through tall trees that guard the forest dark like so many sentinels. A waterhole comes into sight and a Black Rhino appears out of the dense undergrowth, amazingly silent for all its massive bulk. Cape Buffalo arrives to drink and to wallow and a wart hog appears, begins to graze in its unique fashion, on its knees, as though it were a penitent in nature's Cathedral. The shadows lengthen and the marsh birds hurry stiff-legged and a quartet of Bushbucks edge into the clearing.

Suddenly, in the distance, a cracking of tree limbs can be heard, a disembodied sound and one listens, waits, wonders and then, suddenly, the great grey shape appears, a magnificient cow elephant moving with ponderous grace. Then, as if by magic, there are ten great grey forms, then thirty, with calves, materializing out of the twilight to approach

the waterhole. Everything else gives way to the awesome power of these giants. The Bushbuck circle to the outside, the wart hog disappears, the Cape Buffalo snort protest but give way. Marsh mongooses race nearby, a spotted Genet cat appears to stay at a distance, aloof, alert, watching always, all spectators at the magnificient spectacle that is always changing yet forever the same.

Bushbuck - female (Antelope family) (The Ark)

Warthog - A typical grazing position - the comic character of the bush - when trotting briskly along their tails are carried up straight. (The Ark)

Waterhole of the Ark

Mountain Lodge

. . . .passing notes.

The Flame Trees light the way to this place with the Eurphobia and the Candelabra Trees. A Lanner, a member of the Falcon family, watches our progress into a deep forest where, suddenly, Mountain Lodge came into view. A hugh structure, certainly for this part of the world, three stories high and built on pilings, Mountain Lodge offered a breathtaking view of Mt. Kenya, symbol of this complex land, majestic, powerful, awesome, there for all to see yet few to know.

At Mountain Lodge one learns quickly to keep all windows shut because of the Blue monkeys that are all over the forest surrounding the verandahs. In the dense forest surrounding the Lodge, bushy tails and flashes of black and white high in the trees are often the only visual evidence of the Abyssinian Black-and-White Colubus monkeys. However their high-pitched screaming is a constant reminder of the presence. Waterbucks graze quietly while Bush Pigs wander back and forth with private purposefulness and White-tailed Mongooses fly from bush to bush and scamper over forest rocks. A pair of Spotted Hyenas are caught moving nearby in their furtive, slinking manner. They are a reminder that there is danger without beauty, power without majesty and this is indeed a land of many faces, many layers, each with its own fascination.

Cape Buffalo - a heavy Ox-like animal considered very dangerous. (The Ark)

Black Rhinoceros- Smaller than the White Rhino - has no bump on the neck - the upper lip is triangular in shape. (The Ark)

Market place north of Nairobi along the highway

An Acacia tree with Weaver bird nests
hanging off the limbs.
(Tsavo West)

Tsavo West

. . . .passing notes.

Red dirt roads wind through flat, green grasslands and low hills and large rock formations dot the nearby terrain. In the far distance, Mt. Kilimanjaro, the highest in all of Africa, peers down at all that lies beneath it. A water hole near camp attracted a rainbow of

A Vervet Monkey - very common - usually lives in bands. (Tsavo West)

birds, the glossy blue of the Blue Starlings, the vibrant delicacy of the Violet-backed Starling, the soft yet strong gray of the Hornbill, the White Stork, pink bill, white head and white neck and white body except for black tail feathers and the Marabou Stork, black bill with a neck half-black and half-pink and a white body.

In the trees, herds of Baboons fighting and bickering for a

favorite place in the branches and below, a huge Crested Porcupine, each quill as thick as a pen. Cape Buffalo and Elephant wandered down to the waterhole along with Zebra and Waterbucks. Impala, too resting, playing, drinking. They never stop listening, these fleet antelope, never stop being alert and aware, ready to bound away in a split-second.

On the outskirts of the park, Masai Giraffe, Coke's Hartebeeste, Eland, Grant Gazelle and Lion. Amongst the rock formations, the Rock Dassie, Klipspringer, small and delicate as a piece of Dresden China, a vest-pocket antelope that can dart up steep rock with effortless beauty. Ostrich and the Secretary Bird with its long plumes that stick out from the back of its head the way quill pens once stuck out from the ears of office clerks. Despite its name, a member of the hawk family. Fuzzy legs marked the Long Crested Hawk Eagle. At nearby Mazima Springs, Hippos and Crocodiles crowd each other surrounded by a myriad variety of water birds.

To the north, the great black lava fields, some fifty miles in length, at least a mile wide, a primordial reminder, a silent nod to the beginnings of time.

Amboseli National Park

. . . .passing notes.

This place is a place of dust, thick dust and Mt. Kilimanjaro only twenty-eight miles away. A long road leads into Amboseli past hundreds of Giraffe and Zebra and Longinya Swamp. Black Rhino barely visible in deep grass near the lodge. Lake beds dry in the summer but Kioko, a small, lovely lake, had water and a swarm of water birds.

On the dry lake beds, hundreds of Thompson Gazelles, Impala, Gnu or Wildebeeste and Grant Gazelle. Green grass reeds edge the lake, refuge for Egyptian Geese, Sacred Ibis, Blacksmith Plovers and the African Fish Eagle. The reeds also hide the swift and deadly green Mamba.

In the dust, stalking lionesses, some with cubs and Cape Buffalo hunched around trees seeking shade. Across the river there are more trees and grass, the dust vanishing with

suddenness. Oryx and Elephant abound here, as do Crowned Cranes, Purple Heron and the Saddle-bill Stork. Seldom seen Leopard stalk here, while the swift Cheetah prey on gazelle.

Dust and green lushness, divided by the river, a place of contrasts and accomodation where predator and prey adjust and adapt, the eternal balance for survival.

A young calf Elephant nursing - note the breasts are between the front legs - these are Bush Elephants -a species of African Elephant and are distinguished from the Forest Elephant by their larger ears and larger tusks curving outwards. (Amboseli)

A lioness with her cubs. (Amboseli)

Four Cheetah resting after a kill. (Masai - Mara)

Masai Mara

. . . . passing notes.

Green, green and more green . . .the thick carpet of green grass, the towering walls of green trees and then the green made black. They come, migrating, thousands and thousands of them, the Wildebeestes, ungainliest of all antelopes, overwhelming everything in their obliterating march.

Afraid of water, fleeing panic-stricken, driven by forces they neither know nor understand, they trample over each other and all else in their headlong flight. The very plains seem to move with them and others are drawn for their own reason. . . the vultures, the crocodiles, the lions.

But this Masai Mara is a giant game reserve, playground, hunting ground and home for countless more than the seasonal migrators. Hoofed creatures abound, are everywhere, Thompson Gazelle, colloquially known as "Tommies," Impala, Topi, Waterbuck, Grant Gazelles, Cape Buffalo, Zebra. Walking skyscrapers move along the horizon, Masai Giraffes.

A young Spotted Hyena living in a large colony. (Masai - Mara)

Black-Backed Jackal. (Masai - Mara)

Masai Giraffe with a very young baby. (Masai - Mara)

The rivers are hosts to colonies of Hippos, the land to colonies of Hyenas: Warthogs scurry, flag-pole tails poking into the air. Cheetahs so relaxed and lazy whose eyes never stop searching . Black-Backed Jackals and Cape Hunting Dogs.

Elephants, ubiquitous as always, invading camps with impunity. At night, Masai patrols with spears to discourage four-legged intruders in camps. By day, skies alive with wings, swooping, soaring, lighting on water and on branches. . .Blue Herons. . .Marshall Eagles. . . Secretary Birds and Ostrich, Tawny Eagles, Battaleur Eagles, Hammerkopf, Wattled Plover, Egyptian Geese, African Fish Eagle, Malachite Kingfishers, Saddle-bill Storks and through it all, a brown, muddy thread, the Mara River.

Paradise of green, throbbing, teeming, living symbol of Africa.

A pride resting during the heat of the day. (Mesai - Mara)

Thompson's Gazelle - known as "Tommies" are smaller and very graceful, they have a distinct black band on their sides. (Masai - Mara)

Grant's Gazelle - one of the larger and
heavier Gazelles. (Masai - Mara)

"I've got an itch" - Topi - a rather large
Antelope with purple patches. (Masai-Mara)

Common Waterbuck - an Antelope distinguished from the Defassa Waterbuck by a cresent marking on the rump. (Masai - Mara)

Black Rhino in the rain. (Masai - Mara)

The White Bearded Wildebeeste - during migration thousands of them cross into the Mara. They are afraid of water and as a result, hundreds are trampled by others in their haste to get out of the water. (Masai - Mara)

Vultures waiting for a Lion kill of Wildebeeste
- during the migration. (Masai - Mara)

Game Warden and a large Ostrich egg.
(Masai - Mara)

Big Old Crocodile waiting for lunch. (Masai.-Mara)

Two Lioness' stalking Wildebeeste - picking the one on the end of the line, closer, closer - there the lead Lioness striking so fast the Wildebeeste was dead before it hit the ground.

The hunter never letting go of the throat for twenty minutes to be sure it was dead. In a few minutes the male appeared - then the cubs - anything left is fought over by Hyenas

Jackals and Vultures. (Masai-Mara)

Sunset on the Masai - Mara

Samburu

Grevy Zebra - an endangered species seen mainly in Samburu - distinguished from other Zebra by their rounded ears - fine stripes and white bellies. (Samburu)

Impala - of the Antelope family - this variety being the East African is a redder color and has larger horns than its southern cousin. Beautiful lyre - like horns. (Samburu)

Close-up Grevy Zebras (Samburu)

Beisa Oryx - a rather large Antelope. (Samburu)

Male Lion resting after eating his fill of Giraffe. (Samburu)

(opposite page) Vulturine Guinea-Fowl beautiful blue coloring (Samburu)

Samburu

.... passing notes.

Mountains of blue haze that rise out of rocky, sandy soil and dry grass. Thornbushes and Weaver bird nests hanging on Acacia trees in strangely macabre patterns. The Samburu is the home of two uncommon common creatures, the rare Grevy Zebra with its fine, delicate stripes, round ears and white bellies and the Reticulated Giraffe, the most beautifully marked of all varieties of Giraffe.

Antelope abound, all sizes and shapes, the tiny Dik-Dik and the graceful Gerenuk Impala, Waterbuck, Oryx, Grant Gazelle. A river not so much a river as a rippling mass of bodies, the Ewaso Ngiro, awash with Crocodiles. By night, Bush-Babies with their round, liquid eyes, looking not unlike they had stepped out of a Keane painting.

Beauty and cruelty, the special bird-life, Harrier Hawks, Black-Bellied Partridge, Blue-Breasted Beeeaters, Maribou Storks, Yellow-Necked Spurfowl, Kori Bustards and suddenly a lion kill, a giraffe pulled under a bush, stinking in the heat, mother and young ripping, crunching, snarling, the male already full and asleep nearby. Samburu contrasts, a microcosm of this Africa, this land of contrasts. The Go-Away Bird loudly proclaims "go-awayaaaa".

The Reticulated Giraffe - beautiful markings and rich color. (Samburu)

"Upside-Downside" resting in the heat of the day. (Samburu)

A female Ostrich, brown in color, setting on her nest. She usually sets on the nest during the day, while the male - black with white -sets at night. (Samburu)

A nice character. (Samburu)

Dik - Dik, Kirk's long snouted - a tiny antelope being no bigger than
14 to 16 inches. (Samburu)

Two Common Waterbuck fighting over some does. (Samburu)

Cheetah - "In Flight" - the fastest animal in the world has been recorded at over 70 miles per hour for short distances. This one was hunting a Grant Gazelle. (Samburu)

The White-Bellied Go-Away Bird -known further south as a Grey Loerie. So named because of its call. (Samburu)

"The Mongoose Apartment House" - Dwarf Mongoose inhabiting an ant hill. (Samburu)

(far right) Baby Chacma Baboon riding on its mother's back. (Samburu)

Dwarf Galago or "Bush Baby" mostly nocturnal - no bigger than 6 to 8 inches. (Samburu)

Herd of Elephants crossing the river drinking and washing as they go. As they get out -they dust themselves. (Samburu)

Samburu natives

Saddle-Billed Stork. (Samburu)

Crowned Crane (Samburu)

Cheetah - getting ready to go hunting. (Samburu)

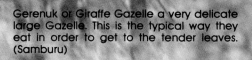

Gerenuk or Giraffe Gazelle a very delicate large Gazelle. This is the typical way they eat in order to get to the tender leaves. (Samburu)

Lake Baringo

. . . . passing notes

A vast lake with an island camp in the center, impressions in isolation. A rough passage, choppy, wind-blown water. Among the passengers, local natives with their supplies, their papyrus rafts towed behind. Smaller islands dot the great lake, each with its own native population and huts, white goats and cattle.

Sunrise and natives singing as they paddle papyrus canoes to go fishing. A true bird sanctuary, a focal point for winged beauty, Goliath Herons, Jacana (Lily Walkers), three varieties of Kingfishers - Pygmy, Pied and Malachite - White-Backed ducks, White-Breasted ducks, White-Faced Tree ducks, ducks of infinite variety, Comorants, White-necked and Long-tailed, Green-backed Herons and Goliath Herons, Fish Eagles and Squacco Herons, African Darters, Pink-Backed Pelicans. Lake Baringo, the heart of the Africa that is feathered, webbed, beaked, the place of so many winged roots.

Dawn on Lake Baringo

African Jacana or Lily-Trotter. It has long toes to support itself on vegetation. (Lake Baringo)

Native boy in his papyrus canoe. He uses small wooden paddles to propel himself. A papyrus canoe lasts about 3 months, then they build a new one. (Lake Baringo)

African Fish Eagle (Lake Baringo)

White-Necked Cormorants drying off. (Lake Baringo)

Waterlily (Lake Baringo)

Botswana

Botswana

. . . .impressions.

Land-locked, yet in the northern part, the Okevango Delta, a place of many rivers with lovely, clear waters, huge, lush, green flood plains and marshes, green islands in the middle of swamps, forests, sand and tsetse flies. Canoes or pontoon boats carry one along the rivers and into the dense papyrus and reeds. Four wheel vehicles take the visitor across the tracks of thick sand. They have names, these magnificent places that are thousands of miles square. . . Chobe National Park, Okevango Swamp, the Moremi Wild Life Park

The great herds are here, the dominant species and the rare ones, as they are up north. But here they are the same, but different. The Elephant is much darker. The Southern Giraffe is buff-colored, the Zebra are the Chapman with their unique "shadow stripes" of buff between the black stripes. The Tsessebe is a lighter edition of the Topi with differing horns.

The bird life ranges from the huge to the tiny, from the Giant Eagle Owl to the Pygmy Kingfisher with a myriad variety of sizes and species in between, ducks, geese, herons, plovers and countless others.

Getting in and out of the camps is by air and brings its own adventures. Landing, one always circles carefully, first, to be sure the game is not right in the plane's path and leaving often necessitates first filling in holes in the airstrip the elephants have made. This Botswana is an adventure for the mind, eye and soul.

San~Ta~Wani

. . . .impressions.

Southernmost of all the camps and right in the swampland. By boat, one poles out through the narrow channels of tall fringed papyrus and reeds as if the world had stood still in primitive beauty. The quick splash of the Lechwe reaches through the reeds and the alert catch a glimpse of a red coat flashing amid the papyrus. Hippos snort and African Fish Eagles scream as they dive for food and everywhere great white Egrets.

A sanctuary, in the truest sense of the word.

Poling through the papyrus and reeds.
(San-ta-wani)

Lioness. (Savuti)

Grevet monkeys. (Savuti)

Savuti

. . . .impressions.

There are two seperate Savuti camps in the Chobe National Park, both on the Savuti Channel. Elephants walk through the camps, bathe in front of them. Cape Buffalo graze in one's ear by night, Lions roar in the not-to-far distance, a Python leaves its marks in the sand.

The animals come in thousands here. The plains are black with game, three thousand Cape Buffalo, a thousand Brindled Wildebeeste, herds of Baboons, great prides of Lion, and in contrast, the solitary hunters, the Leopards.

About three feet tall - a giant Eagle Owl stares down. (Savuti)

Greater Kudo melt into the bush despite their numbers, herds of Chapman Zebra and Impala, Giraffes rising tall above the thick brush, nature's moveable skyscrapers. A rare Sable Antelope permits a quick glimpse and the sharp sound of bones being cracked as the Hyena use their powerful jaws on the remains of a Tsessebe.

But the Savuti is home for the creatures of the air, also. The Giant Eagle Owl waits patiently. The Secretary Bird prances on its stilt-like legs and the Kori Bustard runs almost as fast as it can fly. Ground Hornbills abound as do White-Crowned Shrike, Swenson's Francolins, Yellow-Throated Sand Grouse, Spurwing Geese, Egyptian Geese with their painted eyes and the smaller birds, the Long-Tailed Glossy Starling, the Lilac-Breasted Roller, Chestnut-Backed Finch and Carmine-Breasted Beeeater, a rainbow of feathered life.

A leopard kill hung in a tree some twenty feet high. Very rare, as leopards do not usually kill Hyena. Presumably it was attacking the cubs. (Savuti)

(far right) A spotted Hyena takes a drink. (Savuti)

A Baobab Tree - of great thickness resembling an upside down carrot. (Savuti)

Running in front of Camp - the Savuti Channel where Elephants play and the uprooted trees show this is their territory. (Savuti)

(opposite page) A herd of Chapman Zebras. Note the very large Weaver birds nests in the background. (Savuti)

The Hippo pool. (Savuti)

(opposite page) Brindled Gnu or Wildebeeste.(Savuti)

(inset photo) Crowned Guinea Fowl. (Savuti)

A scratching post. (Savuti)

The Common Waterbuck. (Savuti)

Enjoying the waterhole -Wildebeestes and Impala. (Savuti)

Resting in the shade - a Southern Giraffe. (Savuti)

Close-up of a Southern Giraffe showing many Red-Billed Oxpeckers picking off ticks. (Savuti)

Sunset over the Savuti Channel.

Kwai River

. . . .impressions.

Smoke everywhere, raging forest fires roaring through the land and afterward, blackened soil that magically comes green in two or three weeks. Passing into the Moremi Wild Life Reserve, the ubiquitous Wart-Hogs trot with proprietory air, tails held high in the air. Elephants, Waterbuck, Kudu, Wildebeeste, Baboons and the very rare Cape Hunting Dogs form part of the passing scene.

On the river, Great White Egrets, Dabchicks, Jaconas, African Darters, Squacco Heron, Reed Bucks, Pygmy Geese, Rufus Bellied Heron and hundreds more winged citizens. Driving in another direction the smoke stays thick,

Forest fire. (The Moremi Wild Life Reserve)

matched by the clouds of Tsetse flies and their vicious bites. The fires continue to burn and Giraffes move nervously. A glimpse through the smoke and haze of a rare Slaty Egret standing motionless, waiting, seemingly unphased by all around it.

The car's spotlight finds eyes, red and round, Tree Apes, the Lesser Galago and Bush Babies, the Dwarf Galago. Nightjaws line the road and a Spring Hare darts away. The eyes become yellow, a Serval, interrupted in its feline prowling. The light moves on to catch tall, spotted legs dashing off through the brush, Impala fleeing at the hint of danger.

Watching the fires, the smoke, gazing at the blackened land, one thing is clear above all else. This is a phoenix land that will turn green again in hardly any time at all. Flame is a kind of rebirth. The wildlife watches, waits, flees when necessary. But they know. They are part of the cycle.

Greater Kudu - so well camouflaged. (Moremi)

(opposite page) Near camp - terrible wind and heat. (Kwai River)

Their distinctive ears and different markings are common characteristics of the Hunting Dog. (Moremi)

Close-up of a Cape Hunting Dog - known as the "wolf" of Africa. (Moremi)

(opposite page) Great White Egrets along the Kwai River.

Linyanti

. . . .impressions.

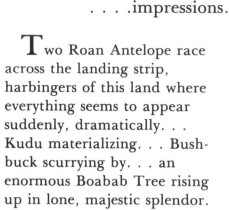

A pair of Red Lechwe - a swamp Antelope. (Linyanti)

Sunrise on the Linyanti River. (Linyanti)

Two Roan Antelope race across the landing strip, harbingers of this land where everything seems to appear suddenly, dramatically. . . Kudu materializing. . . Bush-buck scurrying by. . . an enormous Boabab Tree rising up in lone, majestic splendor.

The camp on the Linyanti River is cool, surrounded by trees where Monkeys and Baboons keep up a constant din as they chatter and fight. Hippos roam around by day and walk boldly into the camp by night.

A wonderful pontoon boat, high enough to allow one to see over the tall papyrus, permits fascinating glimpses of the Sitatunga as they slink away and of the Lechwe grazing. The boat glides silently through the water when suddenly a waving curtain of trunks are lifted high over the tops of the reeds, like so many sinuous, gray flagpoles without banners. The air explodes with the sound of trumpeting as the huge herd of Elephants remain almost invisible behind the papyrus. The boat turns, gives the waving trunks a wide berth.

A surprised Hippo charges the boat. (Linyanti)

A splash hits the water at the edge of the riverbank as a Crocodile propels himself from the land. Among the reeds, a black coil, a Python nest. From deep in the thickness of the papyrus, Hippos roar as they call to each other.

Overhead, and moving in and out of the reeds, the feathered denizens, Reed Cormorants, Pygmy Geese, Pied Kingfishers, Wattled Plovers, Malachite Kingfishers, Black Herons and African Hoopoes, Camine-Breasted Beeeaters and the Little Egret. At dusk, sunsets that seem to try to outdo each other at each day's end, beauty out of the unexpected. . . Linyanti.

Sitatunga - one of the shyest of all the antelope - a true swamp animal having very long hooves to support them on the swampy ground. (Linyanti)

(inset photo) A Carmine-Breasted Beeeater. (Linyanti)

(below) An African Fish Eagle takes off with its prey. (Linyanti)

A group of calves and cows crossing the Linyanti River. (Linyanti)

Mid-river alert! (Linyanti)

Rejoining the herd. (Linyanti)

Late afternoon - Linyanti River

Sunset on the Linyanti River

South Africa

South Africa

. . . .reflections.

The enormity of the country stays, encompasses, absorbs. Magnificent coast lines formed by the Atlantic and the Indian Oceans. In between, desert --mountain -- bush and lush green hills -- red soil and miles of sugar cane -- vast distances punctuated by flowers of infinite beauty. This is the home of the White Rhino, the Nyala and the Blesbok, the Bontebok and the national symbol, the Springbok.

The very names are the sounds of history, born of the land and those who lived on it and came to it. . .Natal. . .Capetown. . .Zululand. . .Transvaal. . .Drackenburg. .Umfolozi. . .Kruger. Today these names play host to the great Game Parks, Game Reserves, National Parks and Game Farms, each distinct in purpose and meaning. In Natal, in Zululand, are four of the Game Reserves, Hluhluwe, Mkuzi, Umfolozi and St. Lucia Coastal Park.

Tree House. (Bona Manzi Game Park)

Hluhluwe, (pronounced Schlu-schlu-wee) smallest of the three hilly inland parks is the home of the rare White Rhino. The Natal Parks Board, responsible for the complete management of these Game Reserves, will, on occasion, ship some of the White Rhino to other parks not only in South Africa but in other countries. By careful work, they have succeeded in bringing these awesome animals back from the brink of disaster. The White Rhino, or Square-lipped Rhinocerous, is a much larger and heavier animal than the Black Rhino. They can weigh as much as five tons! A more pleasant disposition than their cousins, which may not be saying terribly much, they are primarily a grazer whereas the Black Rhino is a browser.

Nyala are found in abundance here, also, Large Antelope resembling a Kudo that has donned a shaggy coat. Males dark brown with orange legs, the females are bright chestnut, smaller and without horns.

Cabbage Tree. (Hluhluwe Game Reserve)

Crowned Eagle. (Mkuzi Game Reserve)

Nyala male. (Hluhluwe Game Reserve)

Nyala female. (Umfolozi Game Reserve)

Umfolozi, largest of the three inland Reserves, does not have as many Rhino or Nyala. Neither does Mkuzi but all offer wonderful "hides" where one can watch the wildlife, furred and feathered, gathered at the various waterholes. Zebra, Kudu, Impala, Giraffe, Wart Hogs and Wildebeestes are among the most frequent visitors to the water holes, along with Monkeys, Baboons, Hadeda Ibis, Grey Heron, Trumpeter and Crowned Hornbills. A pair of Crowned Eagles and a gigantic Monitor Lizard stay large in the memory.

The fourth Game Reserve in Natal, the St. Lucia Coastal Park, is in the St. Lucia Estuary. Jet boats travel the waterways, propellers and gas motors forbidden because of pollution and Hippos. Huge, dark-grey hulks with pink ears form great islands in the water while the knobby green shapes of Crocodiles line the banks, either lying motionless in the sun or suddenly slithering into the water with astonishing speed. Bird life abounds, Goliath Heron, Egret, Ibis, Stilts, Kingfishers, Gulls, Terns, Spoonbills, Avocets and White-Faced Whistling Ducks, to name only a few.

But this is a place of delicate balances, a kind of ecological tightrope where the balance between salt and fresh water must be kept. Salt water making inroads could badly affect the Hippos and their breeding grounds so it is essential that the fresh water from the rivers flows into the channel. An endangered area where a change in balances could destroy yesterday's heritage and today's treasuers.

Goliath Heron. (St. Lucia Coastal Park)

(opposite page) African Spoonbills and a Grey Heron. (St Lucia Coastal Park)

Caught off guard - on land. (St. Lucia Coastal Park)

(opposite page) Hippos and young. (St. Lucia Coastal Park)

Quite a few private, well-run Game Parks exist. They vary in size from three thousand to more than thirty thousand acres. Some permit hunting, but will take guests for game viewing. Night safaries with spotlights provide an opportunity to get a nocturnal view of Leopard, Cheetah, Genets and others. Being face-to-face with a Leopard or a Cheetah in an open vehicle is an interesting experience!

Erythrina or Kaffir Tree.
(Hluhluwe Game Reserve)

(opposite page) Baby Baboons playing in the waterhole. (Mkuzi Game Reserve)

Female White Rhino - known for the longest horn. (Sungulwane Game Park)

Rhino carcass literally covered in Vultures - Cape Vultures, White-Backed and White-Headed, seem to predominate. (Sungulwane Game Park)

Hustling along. (Sungulwane Game Park)

A market en route.

Egyptian Geese. (Umfolozi Game Reserve)

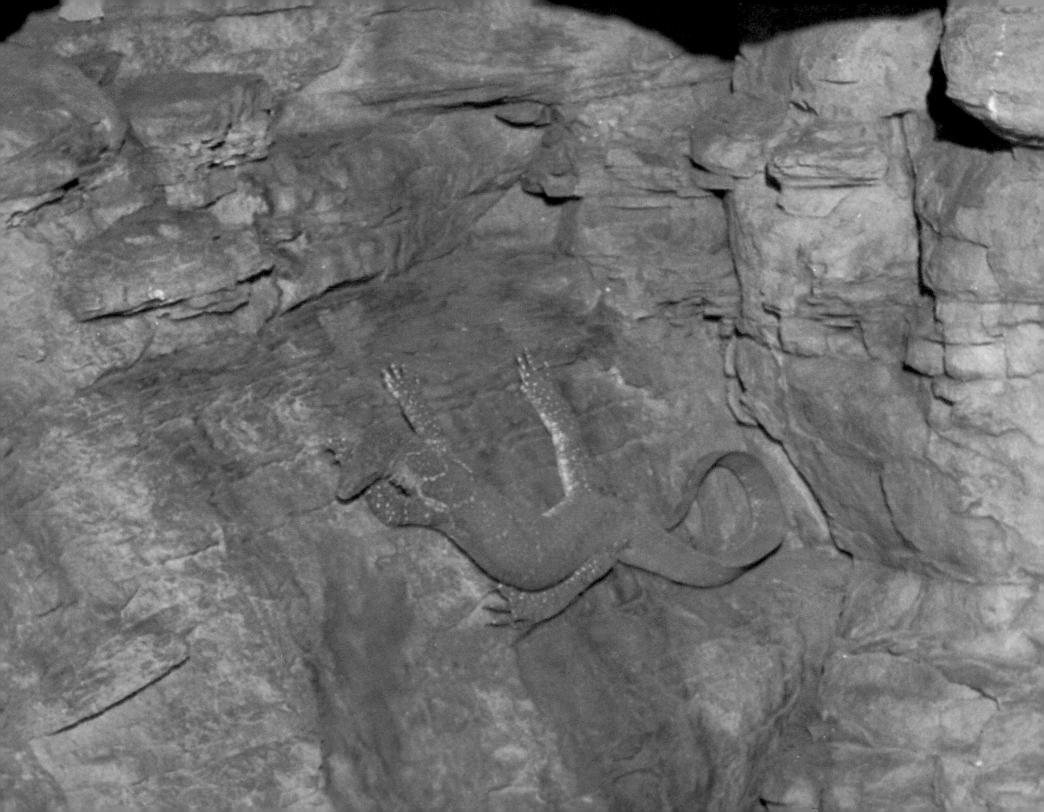

Trumpeter Hornbill on a Cycad or Bread Tree. This tree is one of the oldest plants in the world. (Hluhluwe Game Reserve)

(opposite page) A straight rock wall - 200 feet away - well camouflaged a giant Monitor Lizard. (Umfolozi Game Reserve.)

The mud bath. (Umfolozi Game Reserve)

Close-up of a Southern Giraffe.
(Umfolozi Game Reserve)

(opposite page) Chapman Zebras.
(Umfolozi Game Reserve)

Drying the laundry - along the Garden Route.

Coastline along the Garden Route.

Kruger National Park

. . . .reflections.

On the border of Mozambique in the eastern Transvaal lies Kruger National Park, reaching to the Limpopo River at the border of Zimbabwe at its northern tip. Awesome vastness, two hundred and eighteen miles in length, a refuge for the splendors of a staggering array of wildlife. In Kruger Park, the animals are counted by the thousands and even the rarer species seem to abound. Kruger Park is able to support some 7,500 Elephant, 34,000 Cape Buffalo, 123,000 Impala, 25,000 Zebra, 9,700 Wildebeestes, 10,800 Kudu, 1,000 Reedbuck, 5,000 Giraffe, 3,250 Waterbuck, 2,300 Hippo, 400 Eland, 1,860 Sable Antelope, 340 Roan Antelope, 630 White Rhino, 60 Black Rhino, 1,500 Lion, 600 to 900 Leopard and 250 to 300 Cheetah. Monkeys, Baboons and Wart Hogs simply appear everywhere. In addition, there are known to be over 450 species of birds, 33 of Amphibians and 106 species of Reptiles.

Mr. Broken Tusk. (Kruger National Park)

But a word of caution lest these numbers impart complacency. Despite their numbers, many of these animals are on the endangered list and almost all could cross that fine line between healthy and endangered. Drought, fire and flood, disease and a host of other natural disasters, the greed of poachers and normal attrition, and disruption of the ecological balance, could make these numbers shrink with frightening speed. They exist because of the outstanding work done on all levels by those entrusted with the management of this and other Game Reserves. This includes careful and thorough observation, long-range progams and the strict supervision and enforcement that sees all camp gates are locked at night and no one leaves until the Rangers unlock them in the morning.

Reedbuck. (Kruger National Park)

(inset photo) A side-striped Jackal. (Kruger National Park)

(opposite page) Lions. (Kruger National Park)

Many picnic grounds are scattered along the roads, all staffed and spotless and excellent facilities are the rule at all the camps. But it is always the animals that call, offer a fleeting glimpse of the rare and unusual. The Blesbok is one such creature, a fairly large antelope with striking markings, a white blaze on its face, a white underside and legs partly white, all the rest a nice, glossy brown. The Springbok is another and the Reedbuck, also, the Openbill Stork and the enormous Lappet-faced Vulture were two more I had not come upon before. A place of the unusual, the Kruger National park, Lions mating on land and Hippos in the water, the very many and the very solitary, the massive and the delicate and over all, the sense that here man is trying to preserve his heritage instead of destroying it.

Blue or brindled Wildebeeste.
(Kruger National Park)

African Fish Eagle. (Kruger National Park)

(below) A pool. (Kruger National Park)

A Giraffe's most vulnerable time - drinking - always one or more on guard. (Kruger National Park)

(opposite page) Close-up of a Ground Hornbill. (Kruger National Park.)

Wart Hogs. (Kruger National Park)

Two question marks in the grass. (Kruger National Park)

Sable Antelope. (Kruger National Park)

Red-Billed Hornbill. (Kruger National Park)

(opposite page) What a face - Baboon. (Kruger National Park)

A pair of young-uns.
(Kruger National Park)

(opposite page) A typical water hole
scene - Kudu, Wart Hogs and
Baboons. (Kruger National Park.)

What did you say? (Kruger National Park)

(opposite page) The Greater Kudu. (Tanda Tula Game Park)

A Lilac-Breasted Roller. (Kruger National Park)

(opposite page) Steenbok. (Tanda Tula Game Park)

The Silver backed or Common Jackal.
(Tanda Tula Game Park)

(opposite page) The King of the beasts.
(Kruger National Park)

Monitor Lizard (aquatic).
(Tanda Tula Game Park)

(opposite page) Cape Buffalo.
(Tanda Tula Game Park)

Tanda Tula.

Sunset. (Tanda Tula)

Epilogue

. . . .glancing backwards

It is over. But of course it is not over. It never will be. I keep returning, in pictures and in thoughts. There was so much to absorb, to witness, to draw into oneself. From north of the equator to South Africa's rocky shores, each country was different, special. Every game drive afforded a thrill, whether it was the sight of thousands of Wildebeestes and Cape Buffalo or a solitary Leopard. Whether it was miles upon miles of the green Masai-Mara or the drier areas of the south, the magnificence of Kilimanjaro or the fascination of the Okevango swamps.

I had the feeling of being privileged, of being admitted to a place of special beauties. But not just to observe and enjoy but to go forth and tell, show, bring the message that these treasures can so easily vanish if man does not work to preserve this gift, this heritage. More natural parks and game preserves must be created, the poaching, senseless killing and greed must be stopped.

If dogs were the original excuse for my trips, there are now a thousand more, all the wonderful friends I have made, their hospitality and graciousness, the opportunity to step into yesterday today, but perhaps most of all, to come to understand the problems and the promise of these lands of living treasure. . .this Africa!

Acknowledgements

The Ridgefield Photo Shop, mainly Korky, Don and Jodi, who toiled for many long hours developing, printing and enlarging the pictures, plus hours of advice and help.

Tim Stamp, the Art Director, Ken Thielen, the Publisher, for their time, suggestions and expertise.

My secretary, Jeanette DeFazio, who typed the manuscript, and Karen Schemm, who helped sort and pack the pictures here at home.

Jon Messmann, who spent his valuable hours amongst his own deadlines re-writing and polishing the manuscript.

Thank you all.

Nancy-Carroll Draper